I WANT TO BE A
POSTAL WORKER

By Joanna Brundle

Written by:
Joanna Brundle

Edited by:
William Anthony

Designed by:
Lydia Williams

All facts, statistics, web addresses and URLs in this book were verified as valid and accurate at time of writing. No responsibility for any changes to external websites or references can be accepted by either the author or publis...

CONTENTS

Words that look like <u>this</u> can be found in the glossary on page 24.

HELLO, I'M PENELOPE!

Hello, I'm Penelope! When I grow up, I want to be a postal worker. You could be one too! Let's find out what this job will be like.

4

I want to be a postal worker because making sure that parcels and letters are delivered correctly to my local <u>community</u> is very important work.

Did you know that almost anyone can be a postal worker?

WHAT WILL I DO?

I will collect mail from post boxes, post offices and from businesses. This mail will be taken to a mail centre, ready to be sent out to a delivery office.

Post boxes are emptied at least once a day.

6

At the delivery office, the mail is sorted again into smaller delivery areas. I will have my own <u>delivery round</u>. I will sort the mail into the right order before I deliver it.

Can you see the red vans and lorries that deliver the mail?

7

HOW WILL I HELP PEOPLE?

People often use the internet to talk to one another, but some things still need to be sent by post. These include cards, letters, parcels and gifts.

I will make sure that these things are delivered safely and quickly. Sometimes, someone has to sign their name on a <u>scanner</u> to say that the post has been safely delivered.

Scanner

9

WHERE WILL I WORK?

I might work at a mail centre or delivery office. These are found all across the country. I could also work at a post office, where people can post letters and parcels and buy stamps.

Post boxes are locked to keep the post inside safe.

I might work in a busy city centre or a quiet village. Postal workers collect and deliver mail wherever people live and work, whatever the weather.

WHAT WILL I WEAR?

I will wear a shirt or polo shirt with a fleece or coat. I will also wear trousers, a skirt or shorts. Postal workers often choose shorts, even in cold weather.

Shorts are cool and comfortable.

Hi vis jacket

'Hi vis' is short for high visibility.

Postal workers can walk over 15 kilometres every day, so I will need strong shoes. A brightly coloured jacket, called a hi vis jacket, will help me to be seen clearly.

WHAT EQUIPMENT WILL I USE?

At a mail centre, I will use special equipment that sorts letters from parcels. Other equipment reads <u>postcodes</u> and prints <u>barcodes</u> on mail. The barcodes hold information about where the mail will be delivered.

8 480000 330451

Barcode

Frame

Numbered slots

At a delivery centre, I will use a frame to sort all the mail for my round, house by house. Each house has its own slot in the frame.

HOW WILL I TRAVEL AROUND?

I may use a van to collect and deliver mail. Different sized vans are used, depending on the amount of mail. Large lorries are used to move mail from one mail centre to another.

On my round, I will travel on foot as well as by van. Postal vehicles are becoming more environmentally friendly, so I might drive an electric van or use an electric trike.

I may use a trolley like this to deliver mail.

LET'S HAVE A LOOK
AT POST BOXES

Have a look at your local post box. Does it look like one of these?

Last Collection Time
Monday to Friday
5.00pm

A later collection is made at 7.30pm from the Postbox at Mount Pleasant Mail Centre, Rosebery Avenue

Saturday
11.30a

MON

Post boxes come in lots of shapes and designs.

Most post boxes say when the post will be collected. This shows that the next collection will be on Monday.

Small post boxes like these can be on a post or set into a wall.

After the London **Olympic Games** in 2012, some post boxes were painted gold. This was done in the hometown of every British person who won a gold medal.

WHERE COULD I WORK
AROUND THE WORLD?

I could work at the highest post office in the world. It is at the base of Mount Everest, the world's tallest mountain.

Mount Everest

Countries including Switzerland, China, Singapore and the US are using <u>drones</u> for some deliveries. I'd like to work in one of those countries.

Vanuatu is an island <u>nation</u> in the Pacific Ocean. Off the coast is an underwater post office. Visitors can go scuba diving and post a waterproof postcard home. What a cool place to work!

One of the islands of Vanuatu

A BIRTHDAY CARD'S JOURNEY

A postal worker collects the card.

Auntie Alison posts a birthday card to Andrew.

Happy Birthday, Andrew!

The card is on its way to a mail centre.

The card has been sent to a delivery office. The delivery van is waiting.

Nearly there!

The van is taking the card to Andrew.

GLOSSARY

BARCODES	a group of thick and thin lines that can give information to a machine when scanned
COMMUNITY	a group of people who live and work in the same place
DELIVERY ROUND	the group of houses or businesses to which a postal worker delivers mail each day
DRONES	unmanned aircraft that are flown by remote control
HI VIS JACKET	a jacket with a very bright colour and stripes that reflect light
NATION	a large group of people who share a history, culture or language, and live in the same country or territory
OLYMPIC GAMES	an international sporting event, held every four years
POSTCODES	the groups of numbers and letters that stand for a particular area or street in the postal system
SCANNER	a machine used to read barcodes

INDEX

24